THE
SAMPLER BOOK

OLD SAMPLERS FROM
MUSEUMS AND PRIVATE COLLECTIONS

With 33 colour illustrations and 40 pages of charts

Irmgard Gierl

A & C BLACK · LONDON
LARK BOOKS · ASHEVILLE, NORTH CAROLINA

Contents

English-language edition first published 1987
in Great Britain by
A & C Black (Publishers) Ltd
35 Bedford Row, London WC1R 4JH
ISBN 0–7136–2896–0

and in the United States of America by
Lark Books, a division of Nine Press
50 College Street, Asheville, NC 28801
ISBN 0–937274–32–1
Library of Congress LC 86–82530

Reprinted 1988

© 1984 Süddeutscher Verlag GmbH, Munich
English-language text © 1987 A & C Black (Publishers) Ltd
Stitch appendix © 1987 Lark Books
(Stitch diagrams by courtesy
of DMC Corporation and of Bernie Wolf)

Cover illustration: an American sampler (see page 17)
from the American Museum in Britain, Bath.

Printed in Hong Kong by South China Printing Co.

Historical Introduction

The Sampler Book presents a collection of old embroidered samplers from America, England, Holland and Northern and Southern Germany. They open up before us a world of pictures, often arranged in rows, sometimes composed of whole scenes, but always incorporating the most varied motifs and patterns.

The original name 'samplers' referred to their use as collections of 'samples' or designs for all kinds of needlework. Such designs were subsequently published in book form, and we find the following definition in Zedler's *Universallexikon* of 1739 (Vol. 21, para. 715):

'Sampler is the name given to the cloth on which womenfolk sew neatly and in brightly-coloured threads letters, all kinds of figures, patterns and so forth in many different styles. When the occasion arises, these samplers may serve as patterns, lest some detail should escape the memory.'

Samplers were always filled with motifs from many different sources. They were not merely a collection of borders and lettering but also a reflection of their time: the Gothic and Reformation periods when religion was the hub of life, the Baroque when the focal point became more personal, often with the name or initials of the needlewoman incorporated.

Yet the traditional motifs, whose history can be traced back over the centuries, were still used: tree and stag, bird and sprig of blossom, pomegranate and peacock. The pomegranate was considered an attribute of the gods in ancient times, a symbol of fertility. It appeared on samplers as early as the time of Charlemagne and on Venetian brocades of the 12th and 13th centuries – also on goods imported from the Far East and in the pattern books of the 16th century. Peasant women continued to embroider the corners of their marriage-bed covers and christening pillows with sprigs of flowers. These were symbols of blessing and life which belonged to the world of the Middle Ages when pictorial symbols were more comprehensible and potent than the spoken or written word.

In the 18th century, the variety of objects used as motifs became much greater: there were houses, churches, baskets of flowers and hovering angels as well as the still-fashionable Biblical scenes. Often the sampler was no longer a collection of motifs recorded for future reference but a picture which was either one complete scene or a sequence of widely differing individual scenes. It was surrounded by a border which united the motifs or was edged with a silk ribbon which served as a frame. So it seems that in the 18th century samplers were no longer worked in order to transmit embroidery skills or to collect the greatest possible variety of motifs; they were worked as a demonstration of superbly executed embroidery.

Until the turn of the 18th to 19th centuries, religious motifs from Old and New Testament and later Christian symbols were a major constituent of samplers. Now, in keeping with the changes taking place at the time of the French Revolution, a new style developed from which religious allusions were banished. The colourful saints previously depicted on traditional wooden chests were replaced by vases of flowers, and shrines where miracles were performed were replaced by emblems of the four seasons. The same thing happened to the embroidered motifs on samplers.

Everyday objects came to be used: the woman at the butter churn, a pedlar with his back-pack full of grapes and his little dog at his side, or an elegant lady being carried in a sedan chair by two lackeys (see pages 21 and 22). The brightly-coloured, shimmering silks heighten still further the effect of the merry, exuberant scenes.

All everyday details were thought worthy to be recorded in embroidered form and the tiny stitches enabled the artist to depict pastoral idylls and scenes from the lives of ordinary people. There was such a throng of cockerels, peacocks, squirrels, apple trees and sheaves of flowers that one could almost believe Marie Antoinette's country estate had come to life again! Such vignettes were not limited to European samplers: emigrants took them to America where the skills were cherished and developed so that real little works of art were produced.

Shimmering silk thread tempted the needlewoman to use fine satin stitch which gave full rein to the blending and merging of colours. New fabrics were also used: lightweight woollen or cotton cloth was used as a base, or the finest linens and silks. Small brightly-coloured glass beads were worked in to heighten the effect.

Elegant villas with clusters of trees and flowerbeds were now embroidered, with strolling gentlemen, ladies in Empire-style dresses, fountains, little temples and weeping willows on small hills. Again the sampler reflected the taste of the period; its ideal world emerged in charming little embroidered pictures (see pages 26, 31, 33).

After 1800, a new process was developed in Berlin. Canvas was used as a base: this made counting considerably easier. Printed charts were also used, comparable to those produced today on squared paper (see page 36). Baskets and garlands of flowers, little birds and landscapes, all could now be embroidered on canvas in dyed wools, of many beautiful colours, imported from England. As the charts had to show the shades used, they had to be coloured by hand. Between 1830 and 1840, more than 40,000 such charts are said to have appeared: they were distributed all over the world under the name of Berlinwork or Berlin woolwork. The illustrations on pages 32–35 give a good idea of the charming patterns and bold colours used in the first half of the 19th century.

These examples reflect the taste of the period and the diligence employed by the women involved. They also commemorate the work of needlework teachers who passed on their skills not only to adult enthusiasts but also to little girls between the ages of eight and fourteen.

Just as teachers played their part in the rise to popularity of embroidery, indeed were largely responsible for it, so too they were the cause of its decline. In the middle of the 19th century, Rosalie Scallingfeld of Berlin developed a programme of instruction which was introduced in many parts of Germany and Austria. Barren rows of letters embroidered in Turkey Red thread were now prescribed and this heralded the end of the old random sampler. Up to 1900 these sober labours were an integral part of the standard school curriculum for girls – and then disappeared completely.

Charming samplers of past centuries lie scattered in museums and are hardly accessible. It is even more difficult to discover those that have passed into private collections. It is, therefore, with special pride that we claim to have discovered for this book one or two completely unknown pieces. The purpose of this collection is to bring to life once more some of this work, to show its childlike delight in colour, to reawaken the old exuberance and to evoke the life of the past as shown in the samplers. It is an invitation to readers not only to enjoy the pictures but also to use the charts and to work the pieces for themselves.

Practical Suggestions

The charts in this book are for samplers where stitches are of regular length and are on even-weave fabric where it is easy to count the threads. It is not possible to provide charts for freer forms of embroidery on finely-woven fabric.

You can either follow a chart or use your imagination. If you are in doubt, or have insufficient space for the whole of a sampler from this collection, make your own arrangement of motifs from the chart – a few large ones and a greater number of small ones create the effect which is the special charm of this kind of embroidery.

If you are seeking to give the effect of silk embroidery which is in keeping with certain periods and styles – and very pleasing – it is possible to use six-stranded thread such as DMC. Select all the colours required at the same time so as to achieve a harmonious combination. If you want to make use of thread you already have, take it to the shop where any new thread is to be bought.

It is better to use dark brown than hard black. Most of the colours on old samplers are faded but it is clear that the shades were delicate from the first. For example, not only plain red was used but also peach, reddish purple and rust. In a sampler of 1796 from Salzburg, the embroiderer used the following colours: ivory for faces and hands, light and dark beige, light and dark yellow, brown, blue, green, red-brown and mauve. These shades cannot be represented adequately on the charts. When selecting your colours, use the photographs in this book as a guide. Choose a non-shrink fabric and do not wash it. You can work more easily on fabric which still contains dressing.

The alphabet bands on old samplers vary in colour scheme. All the letters may be the same colour, or every letter a different colour, or every fourth letter dark green, with light beige, yellow and dark beige in between. Or the first letter may be brown, the second light blue, etc. The borders are in two or three colours. Most of the colours have survived, only the black having deteriorated almost everywhere. Only tiny ends or the still visible needle-holes betray the hand of the embroiderer (see page 22). The motif at top right of page 27 suggests how dependent the embroiderer was on patterns: in the absence of an appropriate chart she used her own design and we can see how difficult this was for her. But surely these little irregularities give handwork its charm!

Notes on Illustrations

Embroidery from England with animals and flowers: first half of 17th century ▷

8

Chair cover with flower vase: English, first half of 18th century

Sampler: German, *c* 1710/1720

Detail from sampler opposite

Sampler from Vierlanden, 1741

Detail from sampler above ▷

14

Sampler from Northern Germany (detail): first half of 18th century

Sampler: German, of 1758

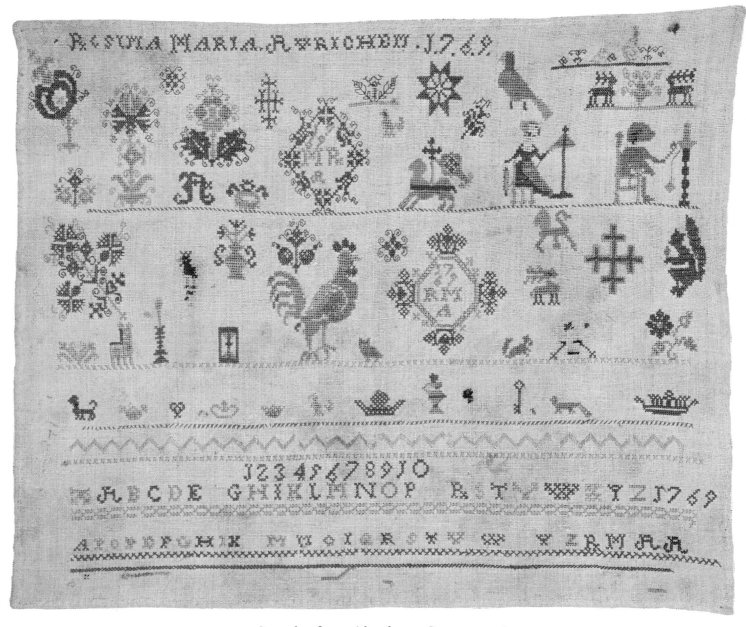

Sampler from Altenburg, Saxony, 1769

Sampler by Hannah Taylor, from Newport, Rhode Island, 1774

Sampler, probably from Erfurt, East Germany, 1777: top half

Sampler, probably from Erfurt, East Germany, 1777: bottom half

Sampler: German, of 1793

Sampler from Salzburg, 1796: detail

Sampler from Salzburg, 1796: detail

Sampler from Saxony, 1796 ▷

Sampler by Jane Ballard, 1799: English work

25

Detail from sampler opposite

Sampler by Anna Sanders, 1801: American work

Sampler from Holland, 1805

28   Sampler by Mary Ann Cook, 1813: English work

Sampler from Holland, 1819

Sampler by Margaret Moss, 1825: American work

Sampler from Brünn, 1828

Sampler from Brünn, 1828: detail from sampler on preceding page

Sampler by Marie Brehm, 1833: Silesian work

Embroidery chart, printed by Hertz and Wegener in Berlin

Sampler from Holland, 1887

Two modern samplers by Margot Irwin: American work

◀ blue	∧ light brown	∷ grey
╱ light blue	● red	╲ yellow
▶ green	○ pink	▲ dark yellow
∨ light green	· beige	– mauve
◤ brown	∷ white	× black

Sampler of 1683 (see page 8)

Sampler of 1683 (see page 8)

Legend:
◄ blue
／ light blue
► green
∨ light green
◄ brown
∧ light brown
● red
○ pink
. beige
:: white
: grey
＼ yellow
◄ dark yellow
– mauve
✕ black

◣ blue	∧ light brown	∶ grey
⁄ light blue	● red	＼ yellow
▶ green	○ pink	▲ dark yellow
∨ light green	∴ beige	− mauve
◀ brown	∷ white	✕ black

Sampler of 1683 (see page 8)

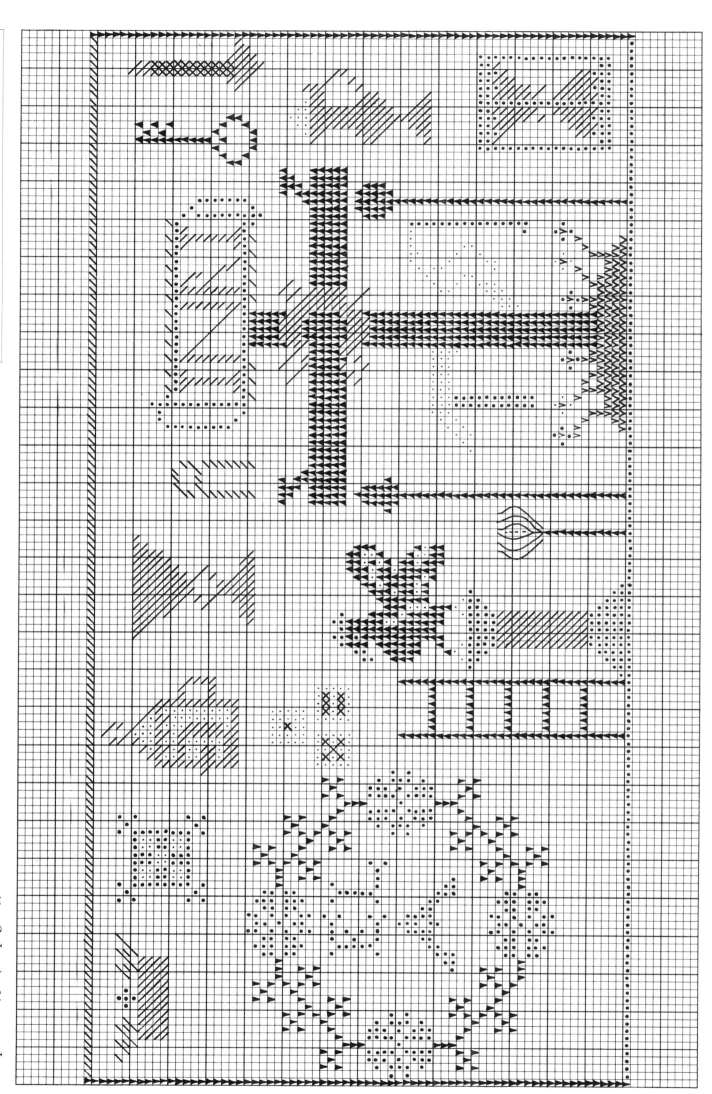

Sampler of 1758 (see page 15)

Legend:

◤ blue   ∧ light brown   : grey
/ light blue   ● red   \ yellow
▶ green   ○ orange   ◢ dark yellow
∨ light green   . beige   – mauve
◀ brown   :: white   × black

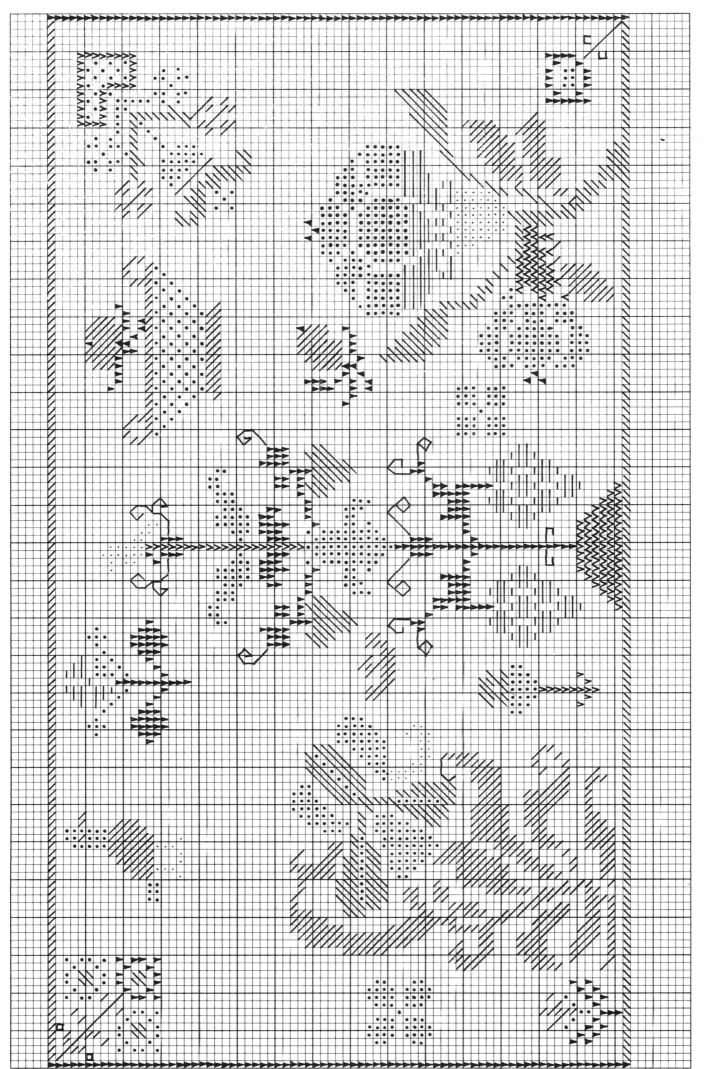

▲	blue	∧ light brown
/	light blue	● red
▶	green	○ orange
∨	light green	. beige
▲	brown	:: white

∷	grey
\	yellow
▲	dark yellow
–	mauve
×	black

Sampler of 1758 (see page 15)

43

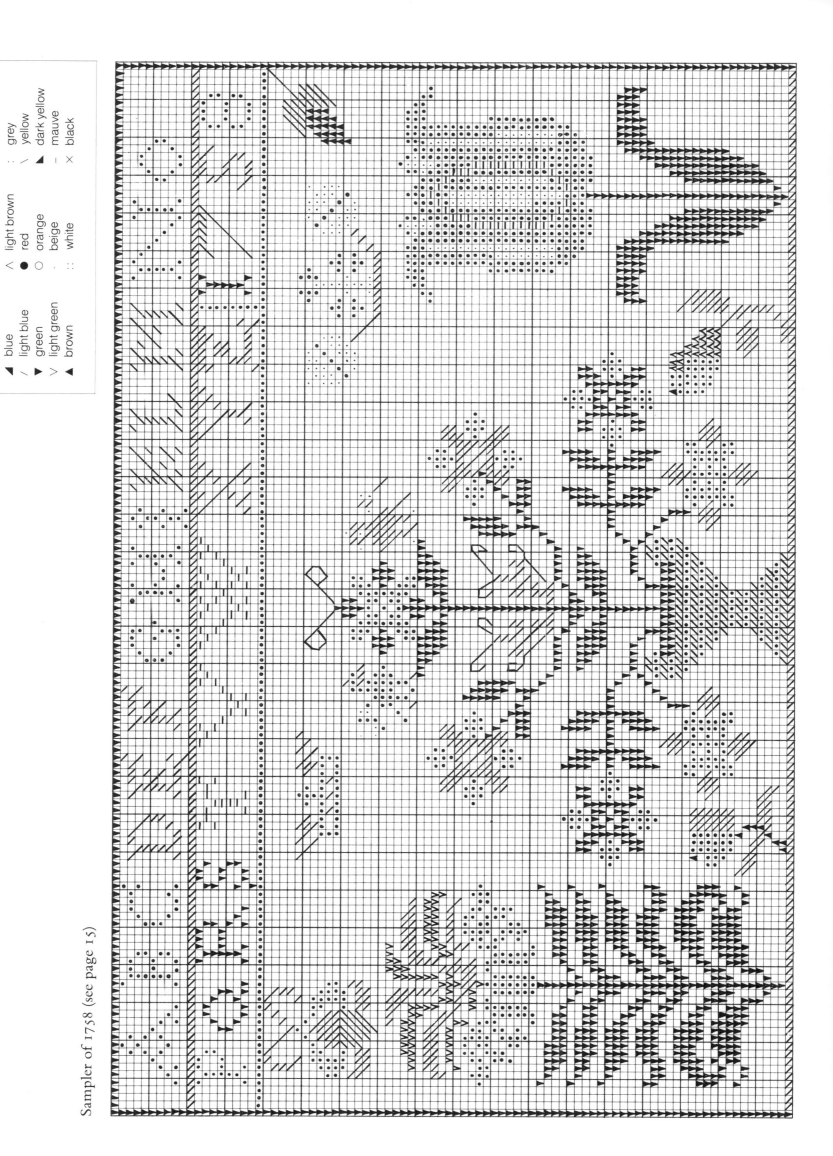

Sampler of 1758 (see page 15)

Legend:

◤	blue	∧	light brown	∶	grey
/	light blue	●	red	\	yellow
▶	green	○	orange	▲	dark yellow
∨	light green	.	beige	–	mauve
◀	brown	∷	white	×	black

Top, sampler of 1819 (see page 29);
Foot, sampler of 1758 (see page 15)

◣	blue	∧	light brown	∶	grey
╱	light blue	●	red	╲	yellow
▶	green	○	orange	▲	dark yellow
∨	light green	·	beige	−	mauve
◢	brown	∷	white	×	black

45

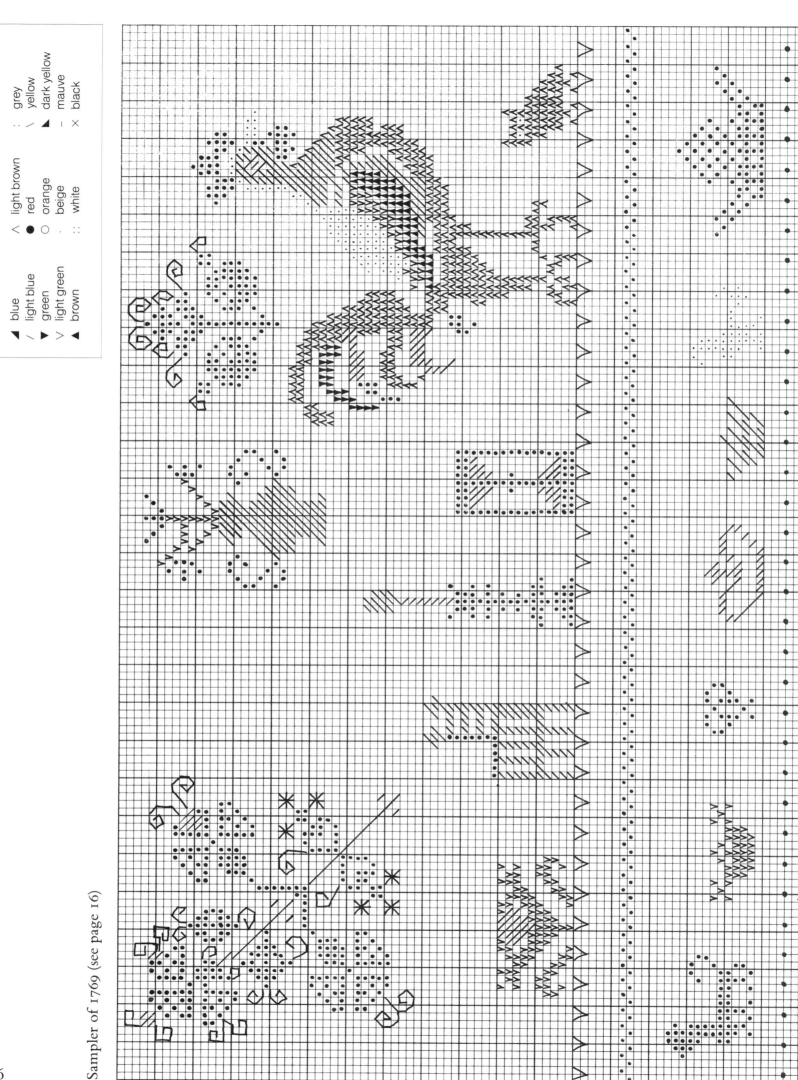

Sampler of 1769 (see page 16)

◢ blue	∧ light brown	∶ grey
/ light blue	● red	∖ yellow
▶ green	○ orange	▲ dark yellow
∨ light green	· beige	− mauve
◀ brown	∷ white	✕ black

Sampler of 1769 (see page 16)

blue
light blue
green
light green
brown

∧ light brown
● red
○ orange
. beige
∷ white

. grey
\ yellow
▲ dark yellow
— mauve
× black

47

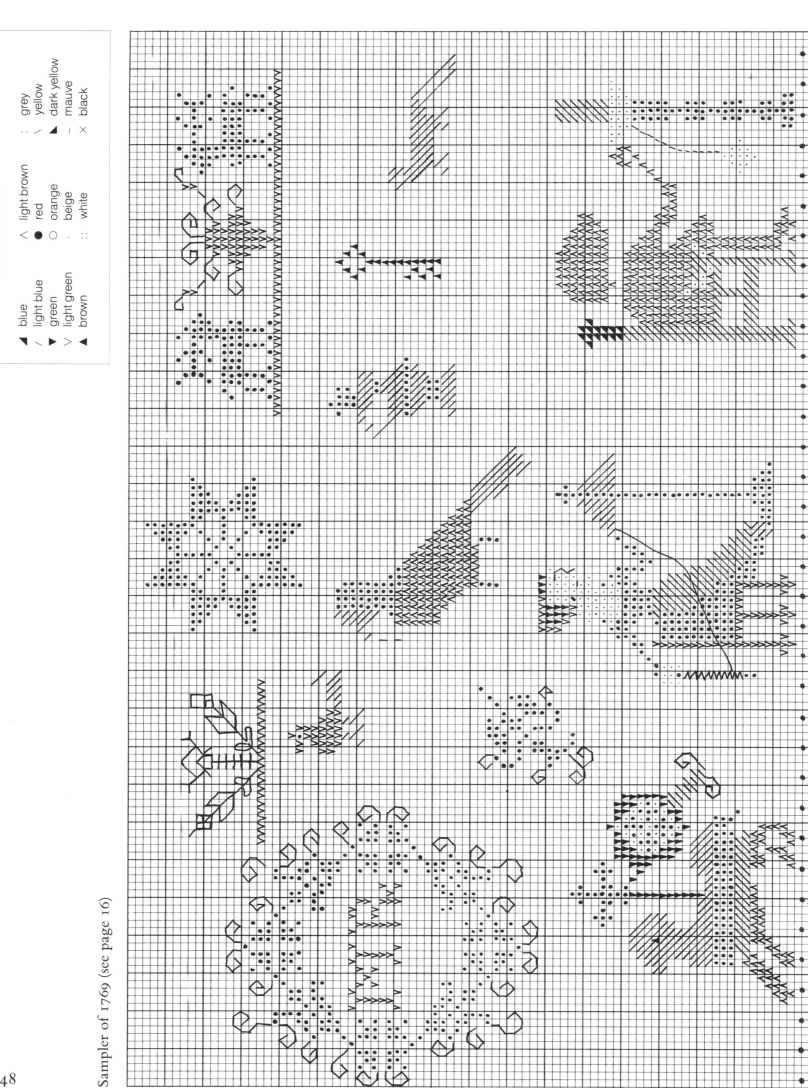

48

Sampler of 1769 (see page 16)

Sampler of 1769 (see page 16)

49

▲ blue
/ light blue
▼ green
∨ light green
▲ brown
∧ light brown
● red
○ pink
· beige
∷ white
: grey
\ yellow
◤ dark yellow
– mauve
× black

Motifs from
samplers of
1793 and 1887
(see pages 20 and 37)

Sampler of 1793
(see page 20)

Steppstich
gelb

blue ◢
light blue /
green ▼
light green V
brown ▲
light brown ∧
red ●
pink ○
beige ·
white ::
grey :
yellow \
dark yellow ◣
mauve −
black ×

Sampler of 1793
(see page 20)

Sampler of 1793
(see page 20)

◢	blue
/	light blue
▼	green
V	light green
▲	brown
∧	light brown
●	red
○	pink
·	beige
∷	white
:	grey
\	yellow
◣	dark yellow
−	mauve
×	black

53

Sampler of 1793
(see page 20)

STRAIGHT
STITCH
LIGHT BLUE

STRAIGHT STITCH
BROWN

54

Sampler of 1793
(see page 20)

◢	blue
/	light blue
▼	green
V	light green
▲	brown
∧	light brown
●	red
○	pink
·	beige
∷	white
⋮	grey
\	yellow
◣	dark yellow
–	mauve
×	black

Sampler of 1793
(see page 20)

	blue
/	light blue
▼	green
∨	light green
▲	brown
∧	light brown
●	red
○	pink
·	beige
::	white
:	grey
\	yellow
◣	dark yellow
–	mauve
×	black

YELLOW

Sampler of 1796 (see page 21)

▲ blue	∧ light brown	: grey	
∕ light blue	● red	∖ yellow	
▶ green	○ flesh colour	▲ dark yellow	
∨ light green	. beige	– mauve	
▲ brown	:: white	× black	

Sampler of 1796 (see page 21)

blue	∧ light brown	: grey
/ light blue	● red	∖ yellow
▶ green	○ orange	▲ dark yellow
∨ light green	. beige	– mauve
◀ brown	:: white	× black

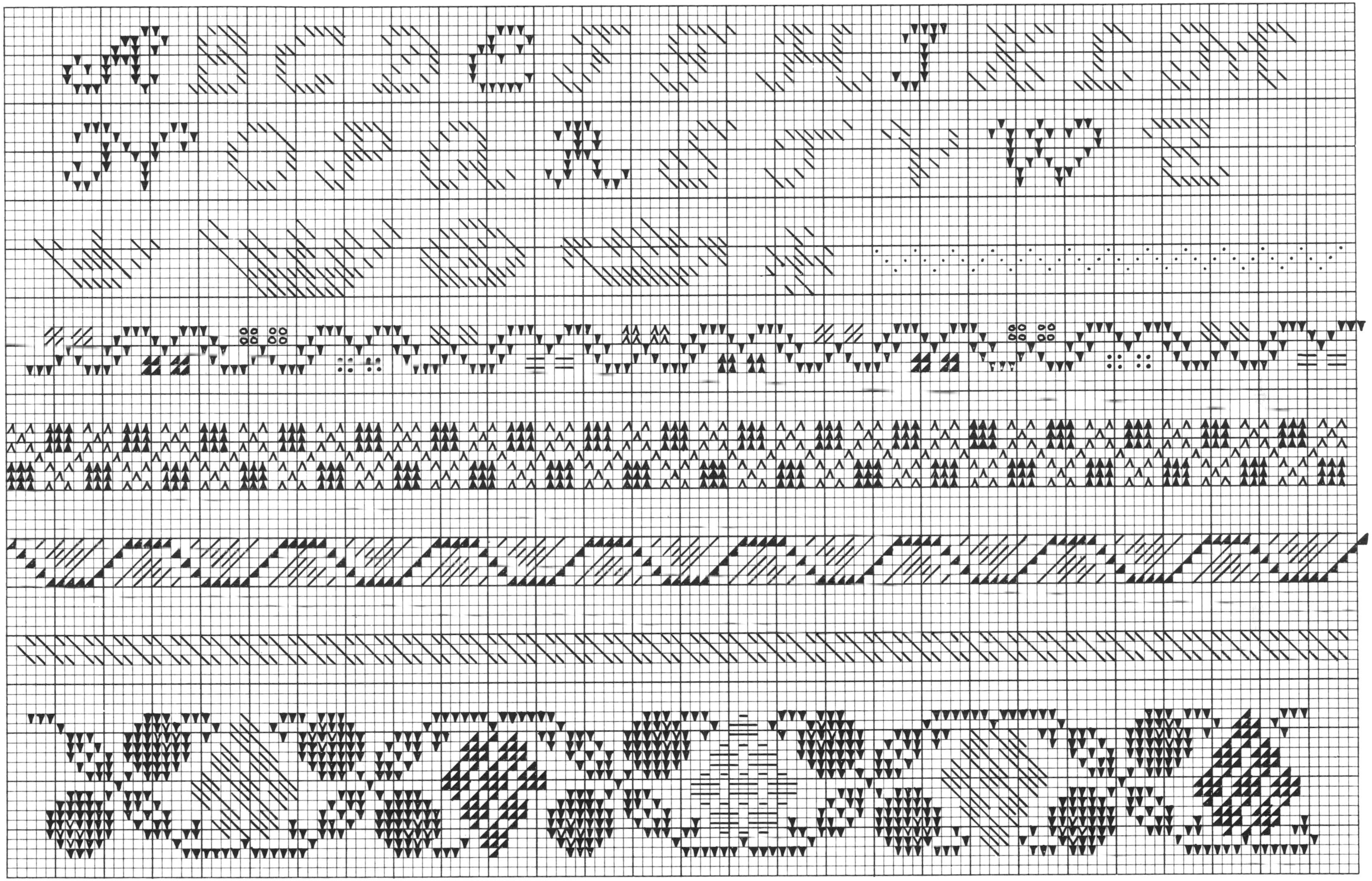

Sampler of 1796

Legend:
- ◢ blue
- / light blue
- ▶ green
- ∨ light green
- ◣ brown
- ∧ light brown
- ● red
- ○ orange
- . beige
- ∷ light green
- ⋮ grey
- \ yellow
- ▲ dark yellow
- – mauve
- × black
- white

59

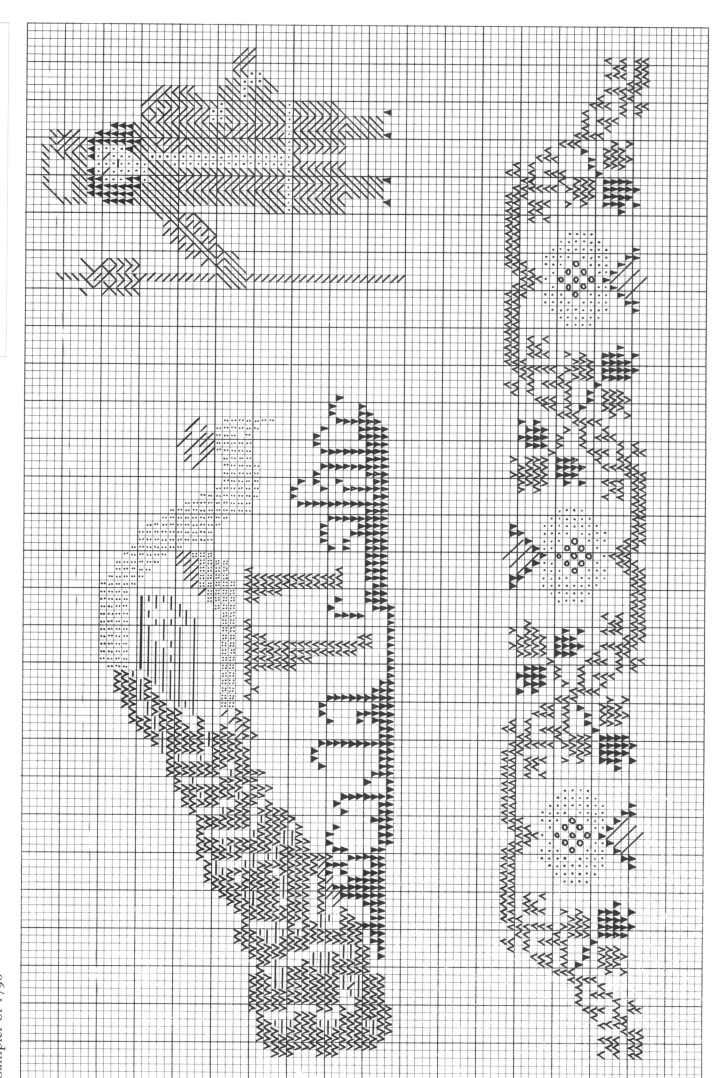

Sampler of 1796

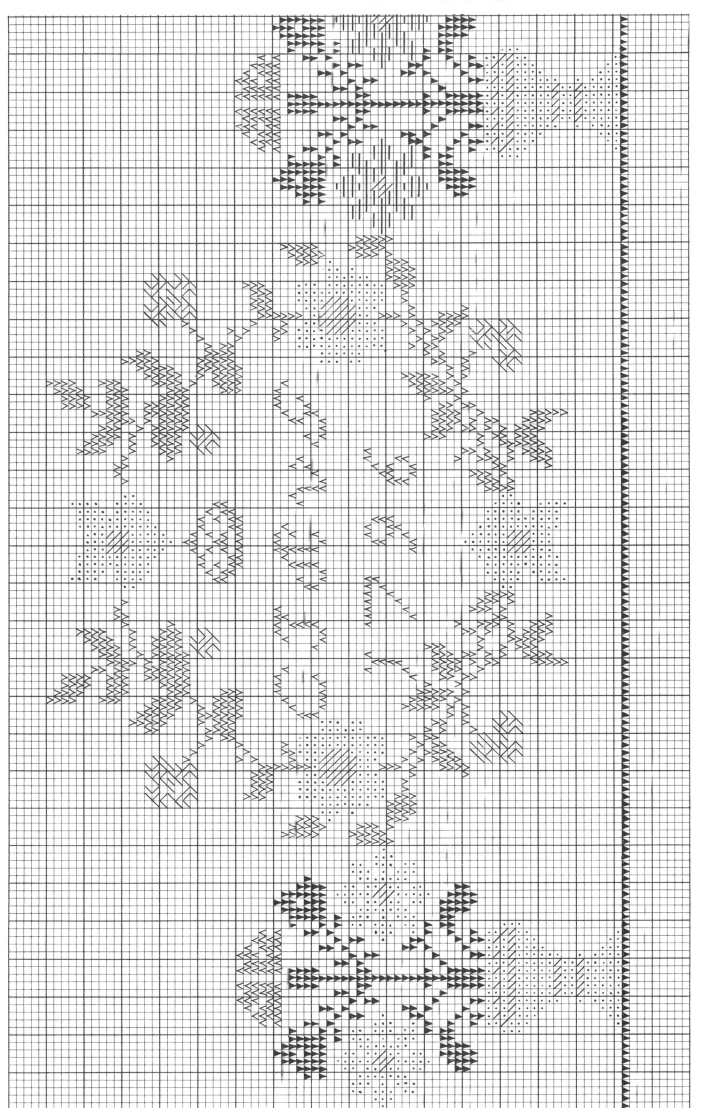

Sampler of 1796 (see page 22)

◢ blue	∧ light brown	:: grey
⁄ light blue	● red	\ yellow
▶ green	○ dark beige	◣ dark yellow
∨ light green	· beige	— mauve
◀ brown	:: white	× black

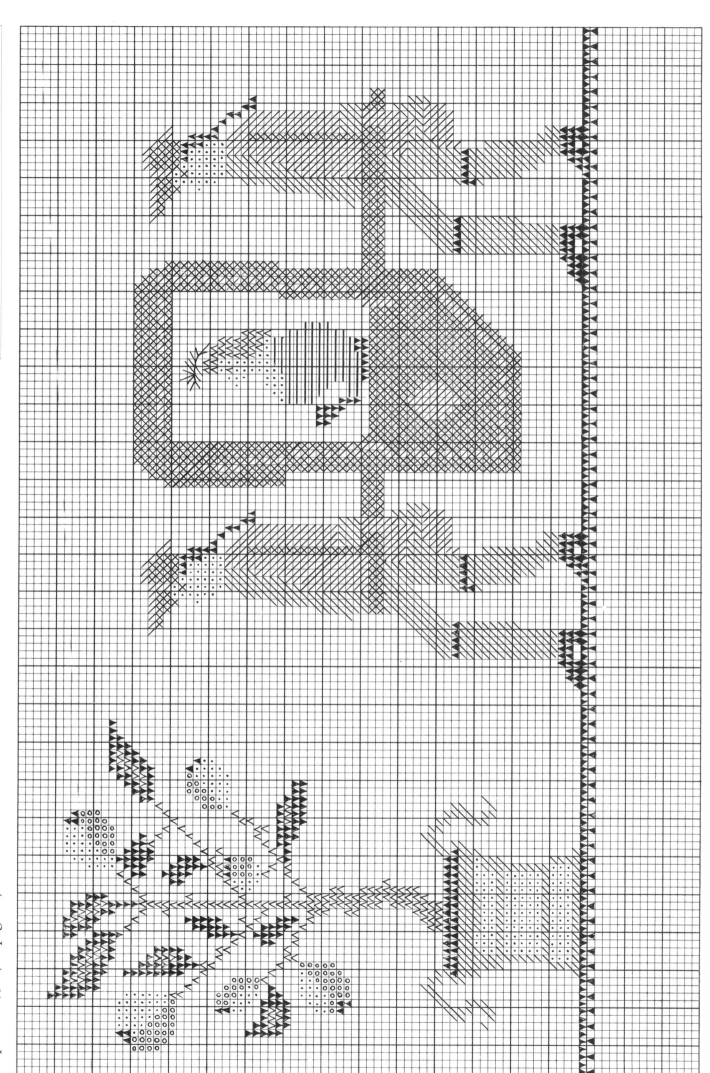

Sampler of 1796 (see page 22)

◀	blue	
/	light blue	
▶	green	
∨	light green	
◀	brown	

∧	light brown	
●	red	
○	pink	
.	ivory	
::	white	

:	grey	
\	yellow	
◀	dark yellow	
–	mauve	
×	black	

Sampler of 1796
(see page 23)

Legend:
◢ blue
/ light blue
▼ green
∨ light green
▲ brown
∧ light brown
● red
○ orange
· beige
:: white
: grey
\ yellow
◣ dark yellow
− mauve
× black

Sampler of 1796
(see page 23)

Symbol	Colour
◢	blue
/	light blue
▼	green
V	light green
▲	brown
∧	light brown
●	red
○	pink
·	beige
::	white
:	grey
\	yellow
◣	dark yellow
−	mauve
×	black

Sampler of 1796
(see page 23)

Legend:
◢ blue
/ light blue
▼ green
∨ light green
▲ brown
∧ light brown
● red
○ orange
· beige
∷ white
: grey
\ yellow
◣ dark yellow
− mauve
× black

Sampler of 1796 (see page 23)

Legend:

◄ blue
╱ light blue
► green
∨ light green
◄ brown

< light brown
● red
○ orange
∙ beige
∷ white

∶ grey
╲ yellow
▲ dark yellow
– mauve
× black

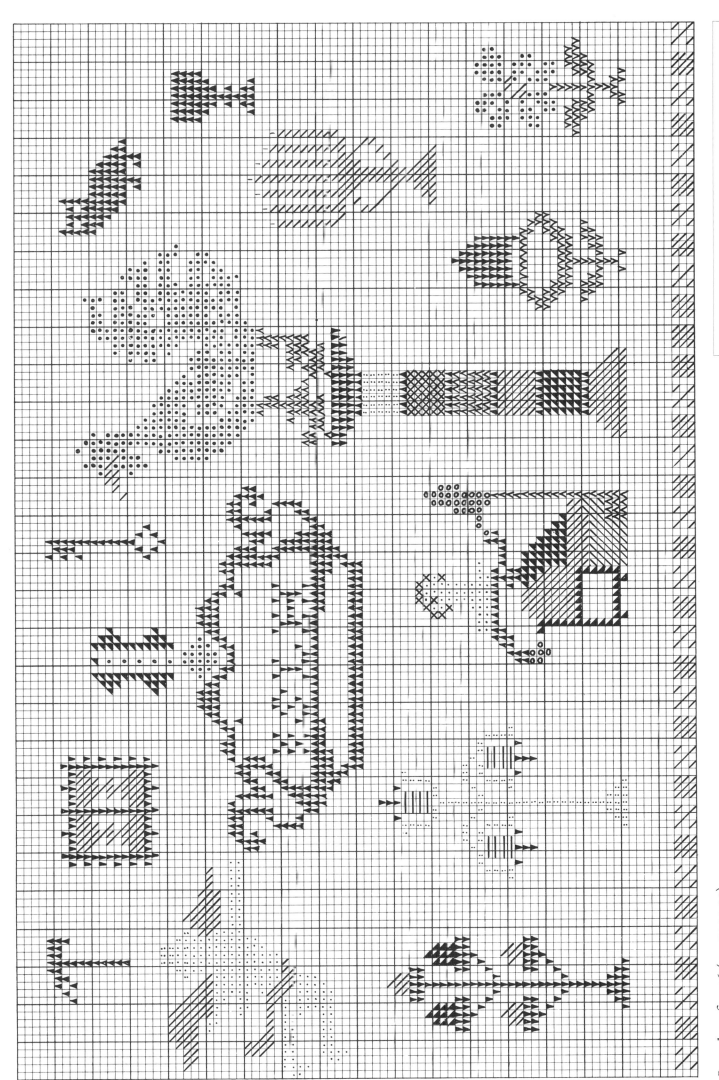

Sampler of 1796 (see page 23)

Legend:

◢	blue	∧	light brown
╱	light blue	●	red
▶	green	○	pale pink
∨	light green	.	beige
◀	brown	::	white

:	grey		
╲	yellow		
◣	dark yellow		
—	mauve		
×	black		

67

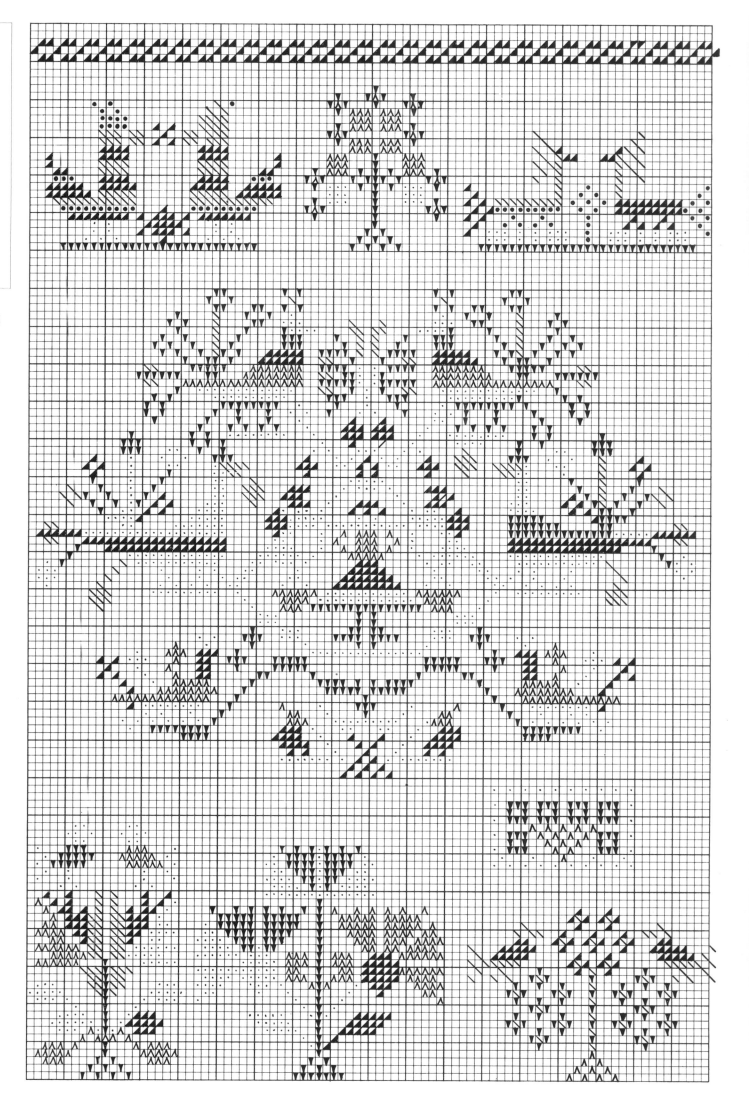

◢	blue
/	light blue
▼	green
∨	light green
▲	brown
∧	light brown
●	red
○	orange
·	beige
∷	white
:	grey
\	yellow
◣	dark yellow
–	mauve
×	black

Sampler of 1805
(see page 27)

Sampler of 1805
(see page 27)

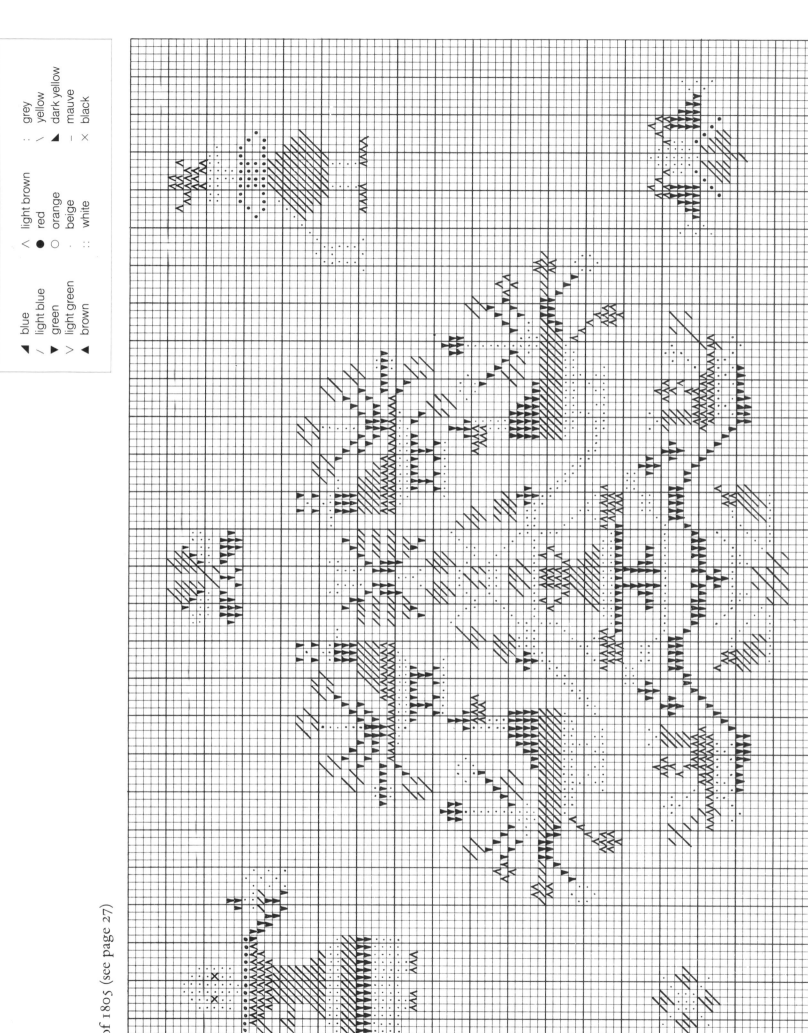

Sampler of 1805 (see page 27)

◄	blue	∧	light brown	: grey
/	light blue	●	red	＼ yellow
►	green	○	orange	▲ dark yellow
∨	light green	.	beige	– mauve
▲	brown	∷	white	× black

◄ blue	∧ light brown	∵ grey
╱ light blue	● red	╲ yellow
► green	○ orange	▲ dark yellow
∨ light green	. beige	– mauve
◄ brown	∷ white	✕ black

Sampler of 1805 (see page 27)

71

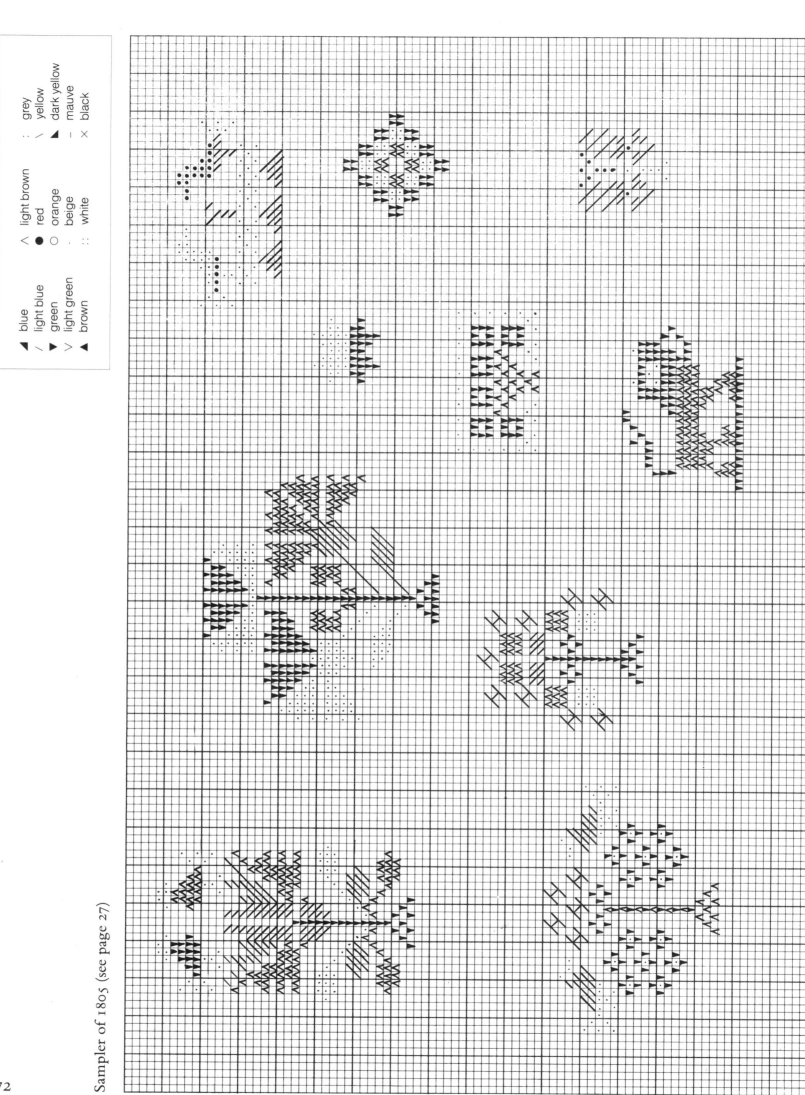

Sampler of 1805 (see page 27)

Sampler of 1819
(see page 29)

Sampler of 1819
(see page 29)

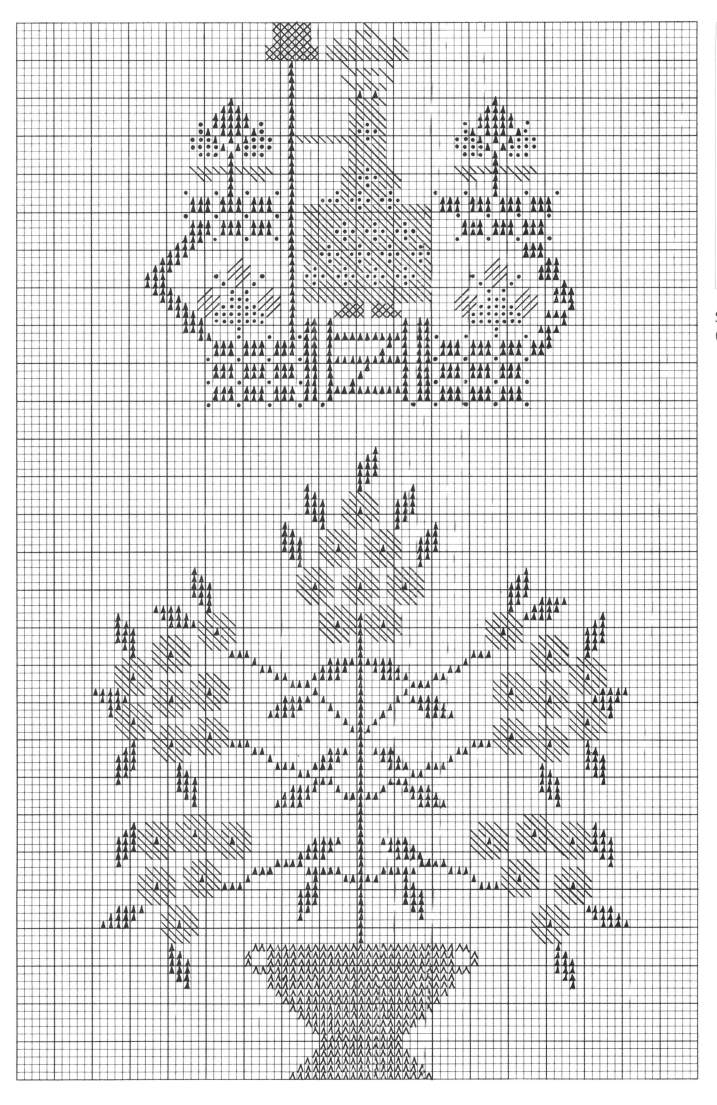

Sampler of 1819
(see page 29)

▲ blue
/ light blue
▼ green
V light green
▲ brown
∧ light brown
● red
○ orange
· beige
∷ white
: grey
\ yellow
◣ dark yellow
- mauve
× black

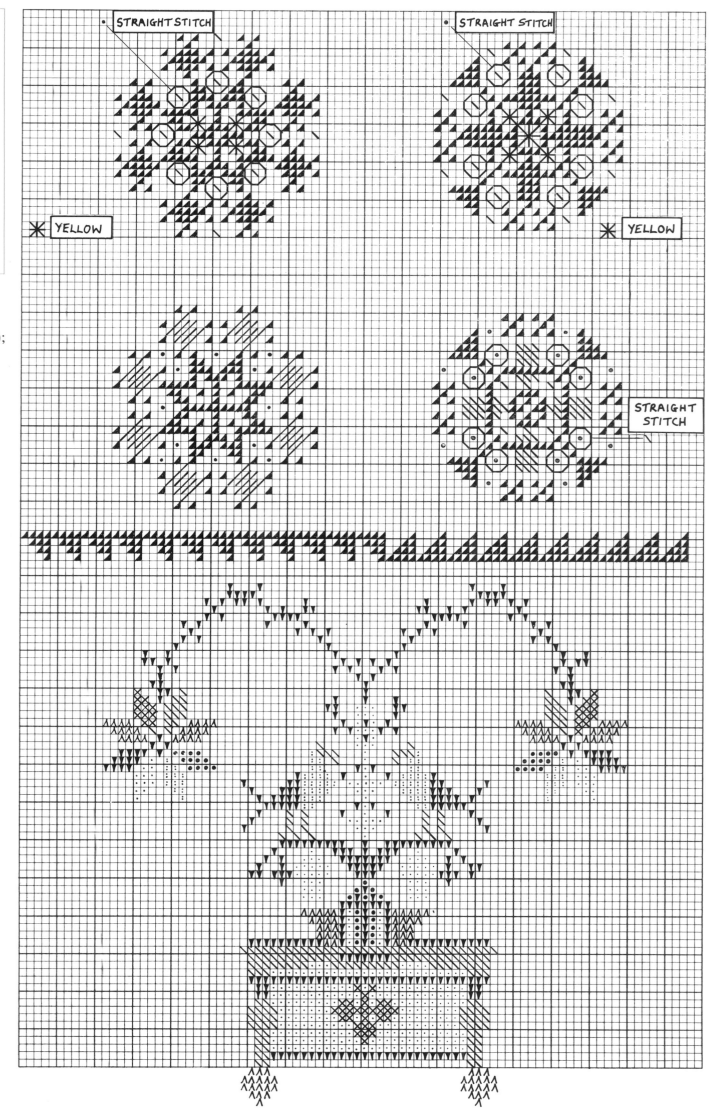

◢	blue
/	light blue
▼	green
∨	light green
▲	brown
∧	light brown
●	red
○	orange
·	beige
::	white
:	grey
\	yellow
◣	dark yellow
–	mauve
×	black

Top,
modern sampler
(see page 38, top);
Foot,
sampler of 1819
(see page 29)

STRAIGHT STITCH

STRAIGHT STITCH

YELLOW

YELLOW

STRAIGHT STITCH

Top,
sampler of 1819
(see page 29);
Foot,
modern sampler
(see page 38, top)

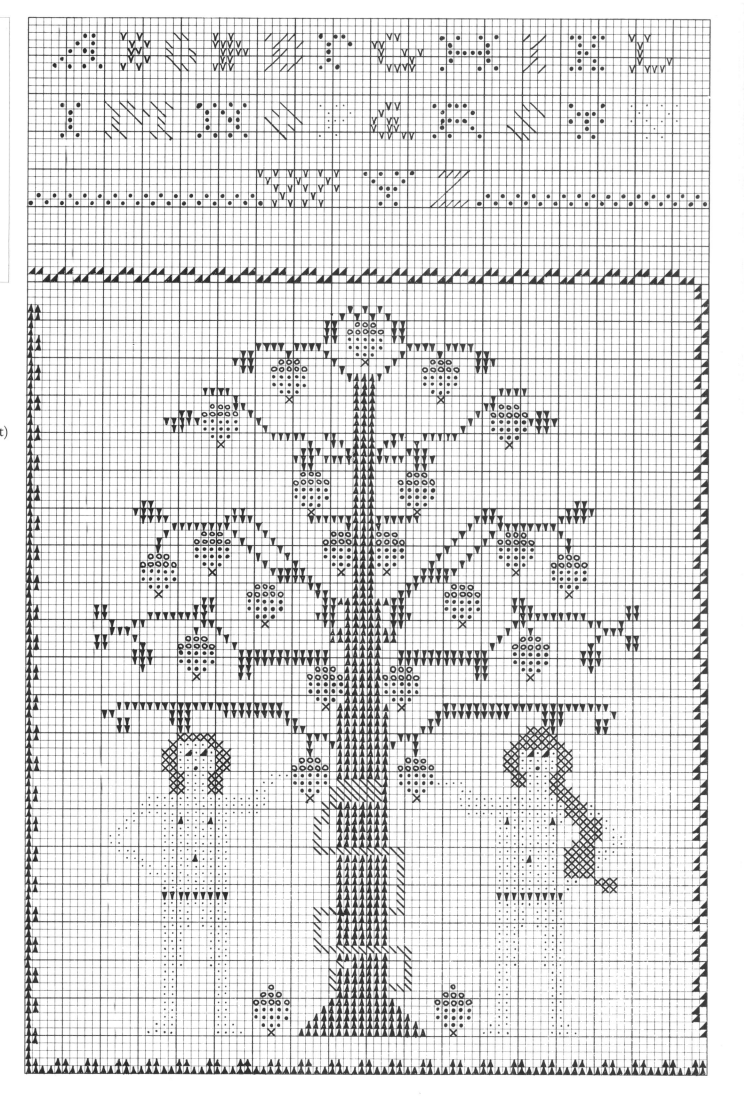

Legend:

▲ blue
/ light blue
▼ green
∨ light green
▲ brown
∧ light brown
● red
○ orange
· flesh colour
∷ white
: grey
\ yellow
◣ dark yellow
– mauve
× black

Top,
alphabet of 1769
(see page 16);
Foot,
Adam and Eve
from modern
sampler
(see page 38, foot)

Stitch Appendix

While there are dozens of embroidery stitches which can be used, it is possible to create a truly beautiful sampler with just a few simple, basic stitches. The diagrams on these pages illustrate stitches often seen in sampler work.

Cross Stitch Perhaps the most popular stitch for sampler work, cross stitch is worked over an even number of vertical and horizontal threads so each finished stitch fills a square. To work it in rows, bring thread to right side of fabric at lower right, insert needle at upper left. Continue working these half crosses to the end of the row. Then working along the row in the other direction, bring needle out at lower left and insert at upper right to complete the crosses. The upper thread of all crosses should lie in the same direction to give a uniform look to the work.

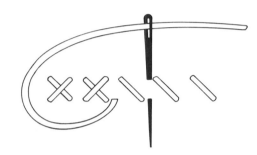

Double Cross Stitch This is a cross stitch which is crossed again. It is worked over an even number of horizontal and vertical threads. Bring needle out to right side and take a diagonal stitch. Then follow the diagrams. The result should be a star contained in a perfect square. As with plain cross stitch, it is important that the final stitch in each cross be in the same direction.

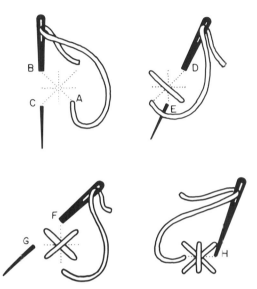

Split Stitch Used either for outlining or filling, it creates a fine, flat surface. Bring needle to right side of fabric at one end of design line, insert needle a short distance away, and bring needle out again, piercing end of previous stitch. Shorten stitch length slightly on curves to make them smoother.

Chain Stitch The chain stitch is useful both for outlining and for filling. Draw (or imagine) a line to be covered. Bring thread to right side at one end of line and hold down with left thumb. Insert needle where it last exited and bring point out a short distance away along line, with thread under tip of needle. Continue, always keeping the working thread beneath needle tip.

Back Stitch The back stitch is used as a basis for many other stitches, and it also works well as an outline stitch. Bring needle to right side along design line, take a small stitch backward along line, and bring needle to right side again in front of first stitch a stitch length away. Continue along the design line, always finishing stitch by inserting needle at point where last stitch began. On even-weave fabrics, the same number of threads should be covered by each stitch.

Stem Stitch Outline with this stitch, or use it to cover lines within a design. Working along a line, bring needle out to right side. Insert needle along line to right, then bring needle back out half a stitch length back. For a wider stitch, angle the needle slightly. Shorten the stitches at curves.

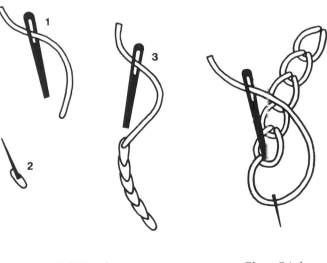

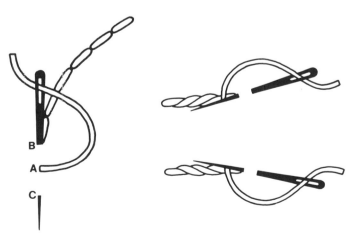

Split Stitch   *Chain Stitch*   *Back Stitch*   *Stem Stitch*

79

Satin Stitches

Satin stitches are useful for filling solid areas of embroidery. The main objective with a satin stitched design is to work flat, even, smooth stitches which completely cover the fabric underneath.

Basic Satin Stitch Begin by bringing needle out at lower side of band to be covered. Insert needle directly about that point and pull thread through. Work next stitch beside first, beginning at lower side of design band. An even satin stitch will be achieved by using a stabbing motion with the needle rather than going from one side of the band to the other in a continuous motion. Take care to make a good edge and not to make stitches too long.

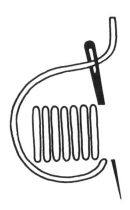

Long and Short Satin Stitch When worked well, this stitch produces a shaded effect and brings dimension to a design. Before beginning, determine the direction stitches will take within a given shape. On a leaf, for example, the stitches would run diagonally upward from either side of the vein line. The petals of a flower would all radiate from the flower's center. The direction of the long and short satin stitch is of prime importance since the flat field it produces will reflect light accordingly. In the first row, alternate long and short stitches along the perimeter of the area to be filled. In subsequent rows, work long stitches, always piercing the end of the stitch above. Fill in the last row with short satin stitches.

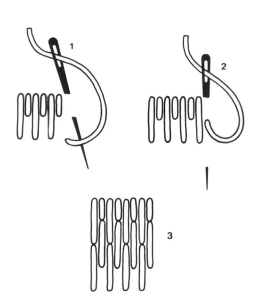

Slanted Satin Stitch This is a good stitch for working curved bands of embroidery, such as letters and numbers. First establish the angle of the slant by taking an initial stitch where it will be the full width of the design band. Then work outward along the band. When work in that direction is complete, return to the point of the beginning stitch and work outward in the other direction. To prevent flattening the angle, take care to insert the needle exactly next to the preceding stitch at upper edge of band and slightly away from preceding stitch at lower edge of band.

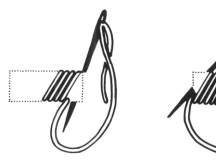

Padded Satin Stitch This stitch gives added dimension to a design feature. To pad, first work outline of the design in split or chain stitch. Next, carefully cover the design area with a horizontal satin stitch, working just to outside edge of padded outline stitching. Then slowly work satin stitch over the design again in a different direction.

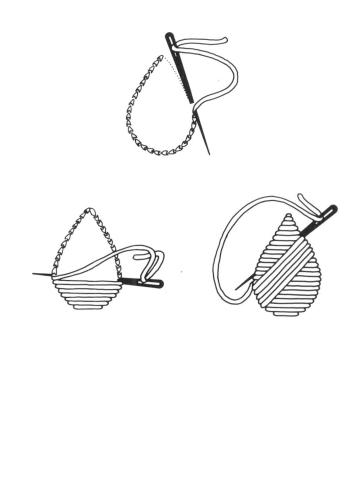